ANIMAL CAMOUFLAGE

ERIN STALEY

Britannica
Educational Publishing

IN ASSOCIATION WITH

ROSEN
EDUCATIONAL SERVICES

Published in 2016 by Britannica Educational Publishing (a trademark of Encyclopædia Britannica, Inc.) in association with The Rosen Publishing Group, Inc.
29 East 21st Street, New York, NY 10010

Distributed exclusively by Rosen Publishing.
To see additional Britannica Educational Publishing titles, go to rosenpublishing.com.

First Edition

Britannica Educational Publishing
J. E. Luebering: Director, Core Reference Group
Mary Rose McCudden: Editor, Britannica Student Encyclopedia

Rosen Publishing
Hope Lourie Killcoyne: Executive Editor
Tracey Baptiste: Editor
Nelson Sá: Art Director
Brian Garvey: Designer
Cindy Reiman: Photography Manager
Sherri Jackson: Photo Researcher

Library of Congress Cataloging-in-Publication Data

Staley, Erin.
What is animal camouflage?/Erin Staley. — First edition.
        pages cm. — (Let's find out! animal life)
Includes bibliographical references and index.
ISBN 978-1-68048-000-9 (library bound) — ISBN 978-1-68048-001-6 (pbk.) —
ISBN 978-1-68048-003-0 (6-pack)
1. Camouflage (Biology) — Juvenile literature. I. Title.
QL759.S73 2014
591.47'2 — dc23
                                                                          2014037750

Manufactured in the United States of America

Cover, p. 1 Rolf Nussbaumer/Getty Images; p. 4 mikeledray/Shutterstock.com; p. 5 Robin Nieuwenkamp/Shutterstock.com; p. 6 Blooozman/Shutterstock.com; p. 7 © Sea Images, Inc/Animals Animals; p. 8 Dmitrijs Mihejevs/Shutterstock.com; p. 9 Gregory Basco/ Visuals Unlimited, Inc./Getty Images; p. 10 zebra0209/Shutterstock.com; p. 11 amit erez/iStock/Thinkstock; p. 12 MVPhoto/Shutterstock .com; p. 13 Reinhard Dirscherl/WaterFrame/Getty Images; p. 14 Mogens Trolle/Shutterstock.com; p. 15 Rich Carey/Shutterstock.com; p. 16 Ryan M. Bolton/Shutterstock.com; p. 17 Art Wolfe/Mint Images/Getty Images; p. 18 Jay Ondreicka/Shutterstock.com; p. 19 E.O./ Shutterstock.com; p. 20 Joost van Uffelen/Moment/Getty Images; p. 21 Christian Musat/Shutterstock.com; p. 22 Bill Curtsinger/National Geographic Image Collection/Getty Images; p. 23 Dante Fenolio/Science Source/Getty Images; p. 24 reptiles4all/Shutterstock.com; p. 25 Sebastian Janicki/Shutterstock.com; p. 26 Gerald C Kelley/Science Source/Getty Images; p. 27 LazyPixel/Brunner Sebastien/Moment/ Getty Images; p. 28 Paul Reeves Photography/Shutterstock.com; p. 29 orlandin/Shutterstock.com; interior pages background image Seiji Nakai/Moment/Getty Images.

Contents

WHAT IS CAMOUFLAGE?

Many animals can hide in plain sight. They do this using camouflage. Camouflage is coloring or patterns that help disguise an animal. This is useful to animals in many ways, and there are many different types of camouflage. Most types help animals blend into their habitats. This allows animals to hide or

This walking stick is hard to see because it looks like part of the branch.

defend themselves from animals that might eat them. The walking stick, for instance, is an insect that looks a lot like a long stick or a twig. It blends so well into its surroundings that hungry animals go right past it.

But camouflage also helps some animals sneak up on their next meal. Big cats have patterned coats that help them to hide from their prey. A lion's light-colored coat blends in perfectly with dry grasslands.

The pattern of spots on this African leopard's coat helps it to stay hidden.

Matching Colors

It is hard to spot the tawny frogmouth. These birds have brown and black feathers that help them to blend into the trees where they live. They perch on a tree branch, close their yellow eyes, and tilt their heads back. They sometimes wait in the tree, motionless, for unsuspecting prey. This form of animal camouflage is background matching. Beneath the ocean's surface are rocks and coral reefs. Among them, you may find the most venomous fish on earth, the stonefish. Stonefish blend in

 If a predator comes near the tawny frogmouth, it stiffens its body like a branch.

This pair of stonefish blend into the coral reefs in the waters of northern Australia.

almost exactly with their surroundings in both texture and color. These patient creatures wait for shrimp or small fish to swim by. Then they open their mouths for a quick meal. Their 13 sharp spines and venomous sacs make sure that other animals don't eat them.

THINK ABOUT IT
How does camouflage help tawny frogmouths and stonefish to be great hunters?

Another transparent fish is this ghost glass catfish. You can see right through its skin.

Flatfish larva use background matching in a different way. They don't have any color. Light passes through their transparent bodies, allowing them to hide in plain sight. Herring also have an interesting way of matching their background. Their silvery scales

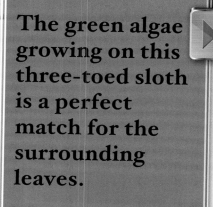

The green algae growing on this three-toed sloth is a perfect match for the surrounding leaves.

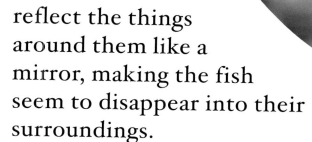

reflect the things around them like a mirror, making the fish seem to disappear into their surroundings.

Some animals get some help from other living things to match their backgrounds. The slow-moving sloth has a shaggy coat that is a perfect habitat for different types of algae. Algae are plantlike organisms. These algae are blue-green in the wet season and brown in the dry season. As the algae grow and cover the sloth's coat, the sloth becomes camouflaged among the trees.

CHANGING COLORS

Some animals match their background by changing the surface of their skin. Both the color and the texture of the skin may change. Texture is how smooth or rough a surface is.

Flounder can change color to match the sand at the bottom of the ocean. Broadclub cuttlefish have skin cells that can change to match the rocks and coral reefs where they live. This keeps them safe

When flounder lie on the ocean floor, they are very hard to spot.

This chameleon waits quietly for prey. When an insect comes by, it will shoot out its tongue for a quick meal.

from most predators and helps them to sneak up on smaller fish.

Some people think chameleons change colors to blend into their surroundings. In fact, color changes depend on such factors as temperature, light, and emotions. Chameleons also change colors to communicate with each other.

COMPARE AND CONTRAST
How does the chameleon use color changes in a different way from other animals?

In addition to changing its fur to match the snow, this hare can move quickly to escape from predators.

In the winter, the fur of the snowshoe hare turns white to match its snowy environment. This keeps the hare hidden from predators. When the snow melts, the hare's fur turns brown. Decorator crabs can match their backgrounds

THINK ABOUT IT

How would animals that live in a desert and animals that live in a swamp use color changes differently?

The day octopus can even hide its dark eye spots from predators and prey.

perfectly because they use the things around them. They are able to attach seaweed, algae, and ocean rubble to their shells. This makes it easy for the crabs to hide.

The day octopus can change both the color and texture of its skin. This is because of the millions of pigment cells it has. The cells shrink and expand to match the color of the background and its texture. When hungry sharks or dolphins swim by, the day octopus can match the nearby rocks. This camouflage also helps the octopus hunt. It can match the ocean floor as it looks for crab, shrimp, and snails to eat.

VOCABULARY

Pigment is a coloring matter in animals and plants, especially in cells or tissues.

PATTERNS THAT TRICK

Some animals have spots and stripes that hide their true shape. These patterns trick the eyes, so it is hard for other animals to see them. This is called **disruptive** coloration. Black-and-white-striped zebras are a perfect example of this. When zebras cluster together, lions have a hard time making out the shape of just one zebra. All they see is a collection of stripes.

> Zebras may look the same, but each has its own striped pattern.

VOCABULARY
Disruptive means causing disorder.

Schools of fish also use disruptive coloration. When a predator is near, fish like herring and cod cluster together. They face the same way and can change direction at the same time. This helps the fish look like one big animal, which keeps hungry animals away. It also makes it hard for a predator to pick out just one.

These chevron barracuda are fast so they can chase smaller fish.

The boa constrictor's skin usually has a pattern of spots and stripes. This design confuses prey as the large snake slithers in tall grasses and along tree branches.

Predators such as tigers, jaguars, and cheetahs have spots and stripes that hide them against the background as they hunt. The pattern of their fur makes them almost invisible. By the time their prey sees them, it's too late.

Giraffes are the tallest living animal, but their colors help them to hide among the trees. Giraffes are covered with brown patchy spots from their long legs to their

The colors of this Madagasca tree boa give it perfect camouflage under the hollows of tree roots.

extended necks. These spots blend in with the colors of the trees and the patterns of shadows in the savanna where they live. Hungry hyenas, lions, leopards, and African wild dogs have to look hard to find them.

Some types of blenny fish have spots that change as the fish moves. The spots help it to match the sponges and algae patches that it swims over.

Giraffes can spot predators from high up, and their camouflage protects them, especially the young.

COPYING COLORS

Some animals have colors and patterns that match those of other creatures. This kind of camouflage is called mimicry.

In some cases mimicry can fool predators into staying away. The harmless scarlet king snake has markings that make it look like the deadly coral snake. The coral snake is the most toxic snake in the United States. Both snakes have striking red, yellow, and black rings, although their color patterns are different. The red rings of the coral snake are next to

This eastern coral snake is venomous. It preys on frogs, lizards, and small snakes.

DID YOU KNOW?
The scarlet king snake is also known as a false coral snake.

If threatened, the elephant hawk-moth caterpillar can make its head bigger. This also makes the false eyes look larger.

the yellow rings. The red rings of the king snake are next to the black rings.

Some animals have spots on their bodies that look like eyes. The four-eye butterfly fish has a large spot on each side of its body that looks like an eye. The extra "eye" may confuse predators. The elephant hawk-moth caterpillar has four false eyes on top of its body. These false eyes make the caterpillar seem larger than it is, which scares away predators.

Some animals use mimicry to prey on other creatures. The tongue of the alligator snapping turtle looks like a worm. The turtle lies in water with its mouth open. When fish come over to get the "worm," the turtle eats them.

Dark and Light Colors

Countershading is when the top of an animal's body is darker than its underbelly. This is a common camouflage for marine animals. When seen from below, these animals blend in with the lighter surface water. When seen from above, their darker colors blend in with shadows on the ocean floor. In both cases, predators and prey have a tough time spotting the animal's true form.

Countershading on this black-tip shark helps it to hide from its next meal of fish, squid, stingrays, or crustaceans.

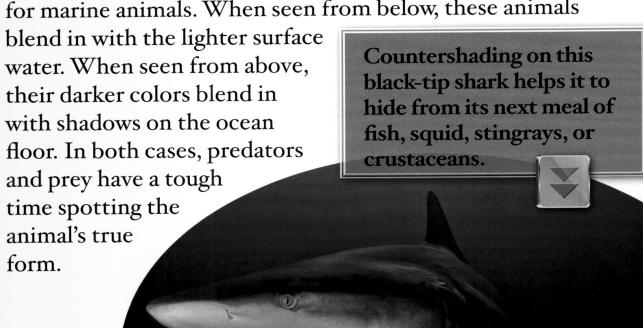

This Humboldt penguin from South America can hide from predators while hunting for sardines.

The countershading on great white sharks, whales, and dolphins helps them to hide from their prey until they are close enough to take a bite. Penguins rely on countershading in two ways. It helps them hunt fish and protect themselves. A penguin's white underbelly is hard to see against the ice in Antarctica, where these birds live. It keeps them hidden from the small fish that they prey on. Countershading also keeps the penguins hidden from hungry seals, sea lions, sharks, and killer whales.

COMPARE AND CONTRAST
How does countershading help sharks and penguins in different ways?

Light and Shadows

Some animals can make their own light. The light and shadows they create is called counterillumination. Some shallow-water squid use light to blend in with moonlight. The cookie-cutter shark produces light that attracts prey. A black band behind its jaw makes the shark look small. When the prey gets close, the fish twists around for a big bite. This form of camouflage is especially effective in the deep ocean, where there is little or no light.

This cookiecutter shark leaves round bites on the body of any prey that gets too close.

The lure at the top of this fish's head glows to attract other fish.

Some sea creatures use chemicals in their bodies to make light. This is called bioluminescence. The deep-sea viperfish has a part that glows and hangs in front of its mouth to draw in prey.

The stoplight loosejaw fish can produce a blue-green light and a red light. Some fish cannot see the color red, so the loosejaw can see its prey without being seen.

> **THINK ABOUT IT**
> In what other ways might animals use their ability to produce light besides camouflage?

COLORS THAT ATTRACT

Some animals use color to attract both predators and prey. This feature is called alluring coloration.

    The blue-tailed skink lizard uses alluring coloration for its own safety. Its bright blue tail attracts predators to just that part of the body. When a predator grabs its tail, the lizard can easily shed it and dart away with all its important body parts still attached.

The long blu tail on this Gran Canar skink make up most of i body length

Sea stars have many arms that attract fast-moving predators. When a predator takes a bite, the sea star can grow a replacement arm.

The orchid mantis uses alluring coloration to attract prey. It looks like a colorful orchid flower. When other insects fly by, the mantis uses its petal-like claws to snatch them out of the air. This insect looks so much like a flower that it can actually attract more bugs than the orchids in its habitat.

Like orchids, orchid mantises can be beautiful colors, including bright pink, purple, yellow, and lime green.

WARNING COLORS

Not all animals use color to hide. Some animals use colors to warn predators. These colors are usually bright (often red, yellow, and orange) or contrasting (black and white). This warning coloration tells predators to stay away or the result could be **toxic**. Warning coloration is nature's way of sounding an alarm.

Under this skunk's tail are glands that can spray a foul-smelling oil up to 10 feet (3 meters) away.

Poison dart frogs like this one are very small. They can be less than 1 inch (2 1/2 centimeters) to about 2 1/2 inches (6 centimeters) long. They come in many bright colors, such as blue, red, gold, yellow, copper, green, and black.

Poison dart frogs stand out in tropical forests. Their beautiful, bright color combinations mean they are highly toxic. One kind of poison frog has enough poison in its skin to kill 10 human adults. Predators see the bright colors and know to stay away.

VOCABULARY
Toxic means poisonous.

The bright orange and black of the monarch butterfly is easy to spot. But some animals know it's best to leave the butterflies alone. Monarchs have a poison in them that comes from eating a plant called milkweed.

The nudibranch, a soft sea slug, has some of the brightest colors and patterns on the planet. The bright colors work in two ways. They allow the animal to hide among the bright coral in the ocean. The colors also warn predators of its poisonous ooze. Nudibranchs eat

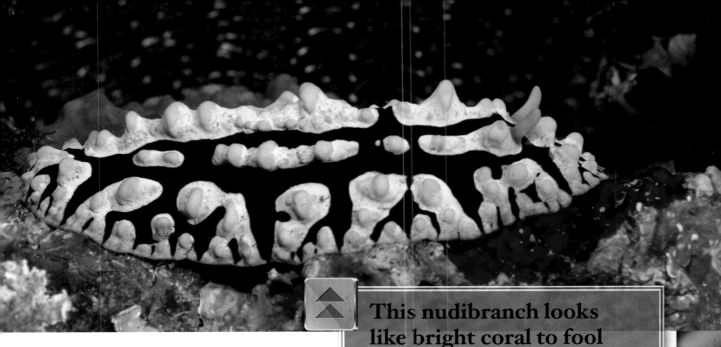

This nudibranch looks like bright coral to fool predators while it feeds on sponges and other small animals.

poisonous animals. They are able to keep that poison in their bodies to use on predators.

Both the bumblebee's and the wasp's yellow and black stripes warn people and other animals to keep away or get stung.

THINK ABOUT IT

Why are warning colors and camouflage both called protective coloration?

Glossary

algae Plantlike organisms such as seaweed.

behavior The way a person or animal acts.

bioluminescence The release of light from living organisms.

cell One of the tiny units that are the basic building blocks of all living things.

defend To protect oneself from an attack.

desert Dry land with few plants and little rainfall.

disguise To change the usual appearance in order to be unnoticed or unrecognized.

habitat The place or type of place where a plant or animal naturally or normally lives or grows.

larva A young often wormlike form (such as a grub or caterpillar) that hatches from the egg of many types of insects.

marine Of or relating to the sea.

mimicry When one living thing resembles a different kind of living thing.

nocturnal Active at night.

predator An animal that lives by killing and eating other animals.

prey An animal hunted or killed by another animal for food.

reflect To give back an image or likeness as if by a mirror.

scales Thin, hard plates that cover the bodies of fish and snakes.

surface The outside of an object or body.

texture The feel and appearance of the surface of something.

transparent Fine or sheer enough to be seen through.

venomous Having or producing poison that can be passed to a victim usually by biting or stinging.

For More Information

Books

Berne, Emma Carlson. *Chameleons: Masters of Disguise!* New York, NY: Powerkids Press, 2013.

Riehecky, Janet. *Camouflage and Mimicry: Weapons and Defenses*. North Mankato, MN: Capstone Press, Inc., 2012.

Schlitt, Christine. *Perfectly Hidden: The Animal Kingdom's Fascinating Camouflage*. New York, NY: Sky Pony Press, 2013.

Schwartz, David, and Yael Schy. *What in the Wild?* Berkeley, CA: Tricycle Press, 2010.

Stevenson, Emma. *Hide-and-Seek Science: Animal Camouflage*. New York, NY: Holiday House, 2014.

Websites

Because of the changing nature of Internet links, Rosen Publishing has developed an online list of websites related to the subject of this book. This site is updated regularly. Please use this link to access this list:

http://www.rosenlinks.com/LFO/Camo

INDEX